Countr

G'DAY
from
AUSTRALIA

C. Manica

G'day!
I'm Kylie
Kangaroo!

G'day, I'm Kane
Kangaroo!

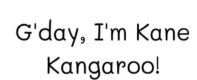

We are going to tell
you about our
country, Australia!

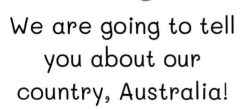

So, where is Australia?

Look at the world map! You can't miss Australia, it's huge!

Australia is the largest country in Oceania, and the sixth largest in the world.

Here are some facts about Australia!

Australia is a federal parliamentary constitutional monarchy.

The head of government is the prime minister, while the head of state is the King of the United Kingdom, who is also the King of Australia.

We celebrate our national day, Australia Day, on January 26.

Our capital is Canberra, in the
Australian Capital Territory.

PARLIAMENT HOUSE, CANBERRA

Our currency is
Australian dollar.

We have a national flower,
the golden wattle.

The green and golden colors of the
flower are the national colors of
Australia.

Australia has six states and
ten territories.

The six states are New South Wales,
Victoria, South Australia, Western
Australia, Queensland, and Tasmania.

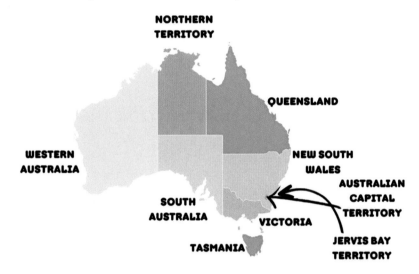

Out of the ten territories, three are
internal territories (Australian Capital
Territory, Jervis Bay Territory, and
Northern Territory). The rest are external,
not located in the Australian mainland.

Should we go and visit some
Australian cities now?

LET'S GO!

Let's visit our capital city, Canberra!

Canberra was founded in 1913. It's an entirely planned city. The area was chosen to be the capital of the country, then designed by architects and engineers before it was built.

Here are some of the famous landmarks in Canberra...

PARLIAMENT HOUSE

NATIONAL CARILLON

AUSTRALIAN WAR MEMORIAL

Now, let's go to Sydney!
Located in the state of New South
Wales, Sydney is probably Australia's
most famous city.

Sydney Opera House
is Australia's most
iconic landmark.

Nearby, there's the
famous Sydney Harbour
Bridge. It's nicknamed
"The Coathanger".
I think you know why!

Taronga Zoo is a
28-hectare (69
acre) zoo located
on the shores of
Sydney Harbour.

Wow, I have
the best
view of
Sydney!

The Royal Botanic Garden Sydney is a great place for a walk and a picnic in the heart of the city!

Darling Harbour is a must-visit place in Sydney. Besides cafes, restaurants, and museums, there are so many attractions there, such as Sydney Aquarium, Chinese Garden of Friendship, and many more...

Sydney is also famous for its beautiful beaches! The closest beach to the city center is the iconic Bondi Beach.

Next, Melbourne!

Melbourne is a vibrant city located in the state of Victoria.

Flinders Street Station is a famous landmark in Melbourne.

Melbourne has the largest tram network in the world!

Most trams in Melbourne are new, but you can still see some older trams, for example the trams used for the free city circle route.

Queen Victoria Market or Vic Market is a great place to buy everything from fresh fruit and vegetables to t-shirts and souvenirs.

Melbourne Gardens is a great place to relax and enjoy nature in the city.

Brighton Beach is where you can find these cute, brightly colored "bathing boxes".

The Great Ocean Road is a stretch of coastline, starts around 100 km (62 mi) from Melbourne. It has amazing views and a lot of attractions along the way.

Let's visit other cities!

Adelaide is in the state
of South Australia.

It's Australia's
festival city, famous
for its many festivals
all year long.

Only a 30 minute-drive from the city,
the Adelaide Hills are a beautiful
countryside with historic villages,
wineries, parks, wildlife sanctuaries,
farms, art galleries, and more!

Perth is in the state of
Western Australia.

It's one of the most
isolated cities in
the world!

Perth has 19 beautiful beaches
with white sand and clear blue
water, all within driving distance
from the city center.

Brisbane is in Queensland, "the sunshine state".

So, it has great weather all year round, perfect for all kinds of outdoor activities!

Some interesting places to visit in Brisbane are: Lone Pine Koala Sanctuary, South Bank, Roma Street Parkland, and Brisbane River (for sightseeing cruises).

Hobart is in the island state of Tasmania.

With Mount Wellington as its back drop, Hobart is known for its beautiful views and well-preserved historic buildings.

Australia is famous for its natural beauty.

The Great Barrier Reef is located off the coast of Queensland. Spanning over 2,300 km (1429 mi), it is the world's largest coral reef system. It provides a safe environment for hundreds of species of fish, coral, and other animals.

Uluru (also known as Ayers Rock) is an iconic Australian landmark located in the Northern Territory.

The red sandstone formation stands 348 meters (1,142 feet) high and is 8 km (5 mi) in circumference. It is considered a sacred site to the Aboriginal people.

Australia has over 11,000 beaches along 60,000 km (37,282 mi) of coastline.

It's not easy to choose the best beaches in Australia, but here are some of the most popular ones...

Bondi Beach, Sydney, NSW. It's easily accessible since it's very close to Sydney's city center.

Surfer's Paradise Beach, Queensland. It's another great city beach. It has golden sand, nice waves, and it's close to shops, cafes, restaurants, and other attractions.

Whitehaven Beach, Whitsunday Islands, Queensland. It has dazzling white sand that swirls with the clear blue water.

Hyams Beach, Jervis Bay. It's said to have the whitest sand in the world!

Bells Beach, Victoria. It's one of Australia's best surf beaches. The longest running surfing competition in the world, the Rip Curl Pro, is held there every year.

Australia is home to some of the most unique wildlife, such as...

koala

quokka

platypus

Tasmanian devil

dingo

wallaby

wombat

echidna

kookaburra

emu

... and kangaroo!

Australia is so big, it has different climates across the country.

The northern part of the country has a tropical climate. The average temperature ranges between 20°C and 35°C (68°F and 95°F) all year long.

The interior of the country has an arid climate. It's very dry there. In summer, the temperature can reach above 40°C (104°F) during the day. In winter, at night the temperature can drop below 0°C (32°F).

The south, southeast, and southwest have a temperate climate. There are four seasons. Average temperatures can still vary between regions.

Australia is in the southern hemisphere, so the four seasons are opposite to those in the northern hemisphere.

Summer in Australia is from December to February, fall is from March to May, winter is from June to August and spring is from September to November.

Australians celebrate Christmas by going to the beach or having a barbecue!

Most Australians are outdoorsy and sporty!

Here are some of the most popular sports in Australia...

With the abundance of amazing beaches, a lot of Aussies enjoy surfing.

Cricket is one of the country's most watched and played sports.

Tennis is another popular sport in Australia. The Australian Open, one of the four Grand Slam tournaments, is held in Melbourne every year.

A lot of Aussies, especially women and girls, love playing netball.

Both rugby league and rugby union are popular in Australia!

A sport that's uniquely Australian is of course Australian football! It's commonly called footy or Aussie rules.

Australia is a multicultural country.

People from all over the world have made Australia their home and have enriched Australian society with their unique cultures, languages, and traditions.

However, the Aboriginal people of Australia have been living in the area for at least 60,000 years. They are among the oldest living culture in the world.

So, you can find foods from all over the world in Australia, but you should try these local favorites!

Fairy bread is a popular treat for birthday parties. It's white bread cut in triangles, spread with butter or margarine, and covered with multicolored sprinkles.

Vegemite toast is as Australian as it gets! Vegemite is a spread made from brewer's yeast. It's salty and full of flavor, so less is more!

Lamingtons are little sponge cakes coated in a layer of chocolate and dessicated coconut.

Meat pies are hand-sized pastry pies filled with diced meat and gravy.

Chicken parmigiana is breaded chicken fillet topped with tomato sauce and cheese.

Pavlova or "pav" is a dessert made with meringue, whipped cream, and fruit.

There's a long running debate between Australia and New Zealand over who invented the pavlova. Either way, pavlova is yummy and you should definitely try it!

So, what do you think?
Would you like to come here
to visit us? Where do you
want to go in Australia?

Bye, see you soon,
we hope!

Collect all the books in the Countries for Kiddies series!

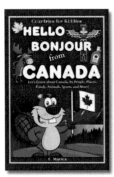

countries-for-kiddies.com

Made in United States
Orlando, FL
30 September 2024